SLEEPLESS NIGHTS
THE NFL: A BUSINESS AND FAMILY

by

Marques Ogden

Cork Publishing

SLEEPLESS NIGHTS, THE NFL: A BUSINESS AND FAMILY
Copyright © 2015 by Marques, Ogden
All rights reserved. Published 2015
Published by VIP Ink Publishing, L.L.C. | vipinkpublishing.com

For information about special discounts for bulk purchases, please contact
VIP Ink Publishing, L.L.C. special sales department at
business@vipinkpublishing.com

Cover Design by Victoria Freeman
Layout Design by Julie Katherine Collier
Photo Cover taken by Ric Moore
ricmoore.com

All rights reserved. Library of Congress Cataloging-in-Publication Data.
Library of Congress Control Number: 2015953078

OGDEN, MARQUES
SLEEPLESS NIGHTS, THE NFL: A BUSINESS AND FAMILY
First Edition Print

ISBN 13: 978-1-939670-05-2
ISBN: 1-939670-05-2
Printed in the USA.

Table Of Contents

3 Mottos I Live by, and Try to Express to Others

1) In Corporate/Business America, revenue means nothing, keep an eye on black vs red; black is profitable, red is losing money. Not paying close attention to this cost me my business and almost my life.

2) Have a strong mind, body, and soul.
Money, Cars, Fame....all of that means nothing. A persons mind, body, and soul makes up the essence of who they are. Have a good health and wellness perspective on life and good things can happen to you and for you.

3) Be a person of FAITH.
Without God in my life I wouldn't have direction.
I lost my faith for a second when my father died, but once I got it back and got on course, life started to get better for me day in and day out!

Chapter 1

My grandfather always told me, "Marques, be something special. Don't let anyone stop you." Football is a huge part of life for the Ogden household, however, it was something that was never forced on my brother, Jonathan, and me. Our father, Shirrel Phillip Ogden, played football for Howard University until an injury during his senior year but whether we played or not, he would always support and encourage us with whatever we did. The sport has been such a big part of our lives, if it weren't for football, my mother Cassandra Sneed Ogden and he wouldn't have met. They met at a football game when she came with one of her girlfriends.

She was attending DC Teachers College, which was right down the road from Howard University. Later on, she became a successful attorney for the Department of Consumer and Regulatory Affairs.

My father became an investment banker for The Federal Loans Home Bank of New York and worked in the trade room of the DC office. When my brother, Jonathan Phillip Ogden, was six years old, I was born at Columbia Hospital for Women in downtown Washington DC on November 15th, 1980. Throughout my baby life until I was a toddler, we lived in Maryland by the University of Maryland. We then moved to a house in Washington DC where I lived until I went to college. We had a fairly comfortable life; both our parents were bringing in enough money and were able to get things we needed as well as what we wanted for birthdays or Christmas. The holidays were either spent at my grandparent's house or at my Aunt Theasa and Uncle James's house that lived 40 minutes away. I went to Stevens Elementary School from kindergarten on up to the 6th grade. I had the same teachers as my brother did years before me, so things seemed to be going really well.

That is until I was 8 years old and a family friend started talking about divorce. I asked my mother if she was going to leave and two weeks later she did. My parents' divorce was my first real influential memory in life, but I had family to take care of me so there was never a huge sense of abandonment at that age. As far as I knew, everything seemed to work out for the best. My father would wake us up in the mornings and drop my brother off at St. Albans High School in North West Washington DC, and then me at Stevens Elementary. After school my grandfather would pick me up and we'd either go to my grandmother's house or the Boys and Girls Club in South East DC. South East DC was infamous for its crime. My grandfather was in the army as well as a boxer trainer, so he was a sharp and tough man. Not to mention he was well respected by the other boxers, and people in the neighborhood. Regardless of what area of town we were in, as long as I was with him I always felt safe. Not only that, but he was a father figure to a lot of kids. He drove a red, late '70s two door Oldsmobile Cutlass and always wore short sleeve polo shirts, khaki pants, tennis shoes, and a hat and glasses.

He was a pioneer in saving lives by trying to keep the youth off the streets and out of gangs. I'll never forget the blood, sweat, and tears he put into that gym. I was taught how to be disciplined, how to exercise, respect women, and be accountable by my grandfather.

As a man and father now, I try to make him proud when I mentor young men and often times find myself giving them the same advice my grandfather gave to me and others. I find a lot of comfort in reliving those afternoons with my granddad. My grandparents were both real strict on my schooling, which helped me develop good study habits. I'd either do my homework at the Boys and Girls Club, or when I got to my grandmother's house. She was a former teacher and would make me study before I had TV time or dinner, which in doing so, ensured I had a 4.0 or a 3.9 grade point average. I did really well. Although despite my studies, I was bullied often because of my weight. I was a big kid, and from the 6th grade to the 9th, I gained a lot of weight. It didn't help on the bullying side that I wasn't popular and struggled socially. Outside of school I had friends, but not so much in school. We didn't have sports, so I felt like I didn't fit in well at all.

Middle school can sometimes be a time where kids may feel they haven't found their style or group and I definitely experienced that, although I knew there was always one person I felt I could relate to more than anyone; my brother. My brother was a big guy also, so I felt like he may have understood how I felt at times. We were both too big to play Pee Wee football, but would be able to play football with the neighborhood kids. Jonathan didn't start playing football officially until he was in the 7th grade at St. Albans. I remember going to Jonathan's football games; he was the biggest guy on the field and seemed like he was in charge. I wanted to be just like him. He was definitely a special player and I'm pretty sure anyone who even watched him play at that age knew he would have a career, but for me, he made me feel special to be his brother and to find something he, as well as myself, could use our size for.

My athletic career started when I was in the 7th grade as well playing basketball. 7th grade on through the 12th I attended St. John's College High School in North West Washington DC from 1992 until 1997.

Being a big guy, my father suggested that football would be the sport for me, however, the 7th and 8th grade classes didn't have a football program. So in 7th grade, I was 5'11" and played basketball for the Silver Spring Blue Devils as a forward. We were an AAU team and had an excellent coach, Robert Jackson. He was big on exercise and would have us run 50 laps each practice; I hated it. We ended up going to the National Championship in Florida when I was 12 years old. Even today Coach Robert Jackson and I keep in touch. He never knew the value of the opportunity he gave me in belonging to a group, learning how to better myself and feeling a part of something bigger. I went on in life to have many coaches throughout my athletic career but Coach Jackson was more than a coach as he was and still is a great leader and mentor for myself as well as the other teammates on my team.

Eight of my teammates went on to play professionally in the NBA or overseas. My friend, Roger Mason, ended up playing for the New Orleans Hornets, LA Clippers, San Antonio Spurs, and several other teams.

We hadn't seen each other in twenty years when we ran into each other in an airport and knew right off who each other were. The friends I made over the years became very influential in my life, like Rick Smith who taught me how to be a better person and develop character. I love reminiscing with them and tell them all to this day how great they were in my life.

While I was developing into an athlete, people started to notice me and thought I could be a potential football player because of my brother's success. When I did eventually want to play, he helped set the road for me; I wanted to be just like my brother. I was never jealous of him, and was always extremely happy for him. He got a lot of praise, but my dad always made sure I knew he was just as proud of me and the achievements I made on or off the field. Our father would always tell us that we had to support and be there for one another. That's exactly what we did and continue to do.

By the 8th grade my brother was already 6'9" and knew he would make it big in football. Colleges like Virginia, Florida, Florida State, Notre Dame, and UCLA were all pushing to recruit him during his high school career.

He chose UCLA and ended up being drafted to the Baltimore Ravens as the number 4 pick overall in the 1996 NFL Draft. Wanting to follow in his footsteps, I was set on being an offensive lineman as well.

I went out for the team when I started high school and made starter on the defensive line as a freshman. Finally, being on the field, I felt accepted, and even today I am still friends with those who were on the team. Playing ball was such a release for me from being bullied. To get where I was, as a 9th grader starting on the football team, I had to work extremely hard, but finally felt focused in doing what I was supposed to be doing. By the time I became a junior I almost quit the team. I wasn't starting on the offensive line like I thought I should be, and we had not gotten to defense in practice yet so I thought I was going to be riding the bench my junior season! I was so mad; mad at the coach because I felt I obviously knew what was best, and mad at myself for not being as good as my brother to be on the offensive line. Little did I know that my coach was using that anger to the team's advantage for the defensive line, and that was where I was slated to start before I threw a temper tantrum, but he felt

I needed to learn how to commit and prove it. I often times have clients who come to me upset about this very thing and I feel I can finally relate to what my coach was creating.

I asked my father what I should do, and he said, "Son, today you'll feel really good that you quit the team and that you told the coach off. It may not bother you tomorrow, or 5, 10, or even 20 years from now, but then you will hate yourself for the rest of your life if you do not go out there tomorrow, go out on that field, show them what you are made of and earn your spot." That was the best advice I ever got. I went back out and worked my way up to starting defense tackle. Little did I know that advice would get me through so many struggles and hardships I would encounter throughout my career on and off the field. By my senior year I made All Conference and was showing potential for my future alma mater, Howard University.

At the end of my senior year I got a call from Steve Wilson, the head coach at Howard University, whom sat down with my mother, father, and me saying, "I watched you play and you'd be an excellent addition to our staff and our team. We'd like to offer you a full scholarship." To my father's surprise, Howard University was the only offer I received. We later discovered that most of the colleges thought I was a junior when I was a senior. I was excited to go to college and to play where my father played, so I felt it would be a great fit. The one on one training from Brad Collins who was a starting offensive lineman at the University of Virginia finally had paid off. He taught me line techniques since my father believed I was more an o-line player than a d-line player. He was a great teacher and taught me as much as he could even though he knew I was going to be playing against his team the first game of my senior year of high school. He still taught me techniques that I couldn't thank him enough for. My brother gave me a lot of great advice too; personally I feel there is no one better to learn from than my own brother for offensive line. I listened to every word he said like it was gold.

I learned a lot about myself in my high school years. My father had a rule that if I didn't make a 3.5 GPA or better, I couldn't play in any games during my senior season.

With that being the bottom line rule, I always knew I had to work hard to achieve my goal. That would definitely be a reoccurring task in so many areas of my adult life later on. My father knew that football wouldn't last forever, and wanted to make sure I was able to get the most out of school and create work ethic to be used in the real world. I was so excited to start college. I felt like I was in my realm. No longer just a chubby boy with not too many friends, I had a team I belonged to, a future to think about and nothing holding me back. Shortly after my freshman year of college, my father was diagnosed with kidney failure. He was overweight and had high blood pressure but I had no idea how serious this was or how it would affect my family forever. He was laid off and had to take dialysis three times a week. I watched him slowly disintegrate, giving up on himself physically and preparing himself for the worst. My dad used most of his savings to put Jonathan and I through high school. He was always trying to better us even at his own expense. He would do without so much so that we had the best opportunities. Now, as a father, I totally understand this mentality. Here's a man that worked hard and would give a stranger the shirt off his back.

Chapter 2

College was something that I always knew I was going to do. I knew that it wasn't all going to be about football, so getting an education was essential. Howard University was the choice for me. In 1998, I had a full scholarship, and due to my father's illness, it was better that I go to Howard as I was closer to home. Wanting to help people, I wanted to become a doctor and chose to major in Pre-med Biology. I enrolled in the summer program, not being able to play since I was redshirted as a freshman, but was able to go to practice. Enrolling for classes was a good way to get to know my classmates and get used to school.

Our first practice was at Greene Stadium. At the time, I was 6'6 and on the offensive line with 15 or 20 of us. Being built, I was highly opinioned of myself, but that was before the vets came in. A week after our first report, the vets had us go to the School of Business, introduce ourselves to the team and tell them where we came from. It, of course, didn't help that I made a horrible first impression. I pretty much knew that I was probably labeled because one, I was big and still learning how to use my weight, so everyone wanted to test me, and 2, I was Jonathan Ogden's little brother, so it was an extra incentive for me to be picked on and shown up. Nonetheless, it's part of the game and this was my time. It was so much easier than what would later entail in the NFL as a rookie.

My offensive line coach, Fred Dean, called me his pup and wanted to work with me the rest of the year. Fred was one of the coaches I wanted to work with; he was a no-nonsense, ass-kicking coach and player. He was once a hog for the Washington Redskins and played in the '80s when Joe Gibbs was the head coach.

I was excited to work so closely to him because I felt I could really learn a lot from someone with his experience and personality. Coach Dean had said that I was going to be one his best players. As a true freshman, he was going to throw me into the wolves early so that I'd get beat and to see if I'd quit or stick it out. They called it Bull in the Ring. At 17 years old I was going up against players like Roy Sampson who was 22, 275 lbs., and 6'9". He had super long arms and was a smart guy. He ended up rushing me, taking me back 5 yards, and then when I landed, my butt landed on my wrist and broke it. At this time, my high opinion of myself changed slightly.

That whole first year was one of my most challenging years because I didn't play. I wanted to get out there so bad but they knew I'd get beat going up against guys who were four or five years older than me. I did get my butt kicked every day in practice, so that only set the tone for me going forward. I was ready to be one of those guys that others had to go against to get better. I was ready to put in the work in practice for the coming years. Overall, my first semester academically speaking was a blur. Juggling between football and classes took me for a ride.

I needed a class on how to be a college student. I had very bad attendance, and was unorganized and unprepared, kind of the typical thing a lot of college freshman experience; too much freedom, and not much experience with priorities. My classes were English, Chemistry, Biology, Biology Lab, and Spanish. It was very difficult compared to how easy it was in high school. At the end of the semester, I ended up with a 1.8 GPA. My father had some friends at Howard and they informed him of my academic situation. My father gave me a choice of getting it together and pulling my grades up, or he'd pull me from college and I'd have to come home and get a job. I told him he couldn't do that because he wasn't paying for my college. For starters, no matter what age or size, or how sick he was, I should have known that he would smack the words right out of my mouth for saying that. He then proceeded to explain that he can do whatever he wants and wasn't going to let me waste Howard's money ($125,000) or my education. So, after regaining feeling in my face, I figured I might need to get a better handle of the college life. I came back to school the next semester and switched majors to Finance to have classes like Economics, Math, and Algebra.

In doing so, I brought my GPA up to a 4.0 but I still had to go to summer school to make up the work I missed. Along the way I had amazing help from my advisors in counseling as I made the transition between majors. Howard has amazing educators who really help their students find their strengths and use them to create a potential field of study. My counselors helped in teaching me how to plan out a timeline and getting me where I needed to be. I was able to utilize the administrators' help to set goals and objectives to where I wanted to be with my education and future. During this time my father wasn't dealing well with his kidney treatments. There were issues where his body wasn't reacting well to them. I struggled seeing him that way and lucky enough, the hospital was only five minutes away from the school. Spending so much time with him, I sacrificed training some to be with him, much to his dismay. I was still working hard though and hoping to get to play the next year. My offensive line coach brought it to my attention that coming back that semester, I was going to be a starting lineman. I was so excited! This was what I had been working so hard for; the opportunity to be a starting offensive lineman at Howard University.

Our line was a senior left tackle, senior left guard, junior center, senior right guard, and me, right tackle as a redshirt freshman. The position was pretty difficult and at the same time very exciting. My job was blocking pass rushers. Like math, football is about angles, degrees, leverage, and placement. If you can understand math you can understand football. Understanding football is only half of the equation though; the other half is about playing the game. Our first game was in Jackson, Mississippi against Jackson State where it was 100 degrees even at night. It didn't help that I was 330 lbs., so to me it was super-hot. The game couldn't have gone any worse than it already had.

I was so nervous that first game. I just wanted to get it over with and under my belt. I went up against players who outranked me; I was beat like a drum and gave up four sacks in my first college game. My problem was that I dwelled on the past and in that got beat more often instead of keeping my head up and moving forward. That being said, we lost our second game as well, but I played better and gave myself and the team respect and proof that I could play. With the game you'd have wins and you'd have losses, as well as ups and downs, but you'd have to learn to play like a professional. Attending Howard, they did a really great job in preparing me for life after college. I have maintained close relations with staff that helped me through my college years, such as Pastor Isaiah Harvin who still keeps me accountable for decisions I make in life. I learned that it was really hard watching what you eat, having weight training, going to class, and being academically eligible to maintain my scholarship all the while juggling family life. I loved my classes, but learned fairly quickly how every teacher is not going to like you, nor will every teacher be a football fan. At first, this was very difficult for me to understand. Who doesn't love football?

Coming back over the summer in my junior year I lost 35 lbs. and now weighed 305. My mind was set on giving it my all and having my best football year yet. Not to mention I was now considered a veteran in my coach's eyes, which was good because we were now able to live in the Towers on George Ave. Living in the Towers, we weren't under the coach's supervision and were given a feeling of a higher level of maturity.

In doing so, this gave me the opportunity to gain some independence. It was also a co-ed dorm of both athletes and students, which opened up a whole new side to life that definitely wasn't about football.

My father seemed to be getting his appearance back, but soon deteriorated rather quickly. He was taking treatments again, but losing way too much weight. I didn't understand what was going on, but I was angry about it. I needed my dad to be healthy. I took it really hard and ended up getting into a verbal confrontation with a coach. I should've known better, but luckily the altercation only got me suspended for a game and a half, and I was sent to counseling. I didn't understand my feelings or how to control them. I was angry and no matter all the things that were going well, my father, who was my support in life, was ailing. On the field I was playing right tackle once again and I was looked at as a leader, but I let myself, and my team down. It was like a lightbulb had gone off that I couldn't go through life mad at the world; I wasn't useful to myself or anyone around me if I was angry. My coach wanted me back on the field, and I was ready to be back and channel my anger into the game.

Apparently I did it so well, I ended up making the Second Team All-Conference, and Pre Season All American for that upcoming year. I was finding ways to enjoy and excel at football but still create goals for life after college as well. I took on an internship with Merrill Lynch working under Al Korben handling blue chip stock accounts and networking. I liked working with people and wanted to be a stockbroker after college if football didn't work out. I managed to finish my last two years playing left tackle and center, keeping my academics stable and proud that my dad was able to attend every college game I ever had. I was ready for what was next with my football career. I enjoyed time with my family and close friends. I feel in life you have a lot of associates but only a few real, protective, close friends. I learned that I had that at this time. I had my friends who saw my struggle and hard work. They were so protective and supportive of my dreams just about as much as I was. I remember one night being at a nightclub, enjoying the weekend with a group of friends. Somehow, a fight started and for some reason, me being big, people always wanted to start something with me to show off. My friend, Darrick, shuffled me out of that place so fast.

He just kept saying, "You can't mess up your draft status, you can't get in trouble. I'll handle it!" He was so protective of me and had my best interest at heart even at that time. He's still one of my closest friends and is now my youngest daughter's Godfather. It seems wherever life may take you, if you have those solid few people in your crew, you have found something very valuable.

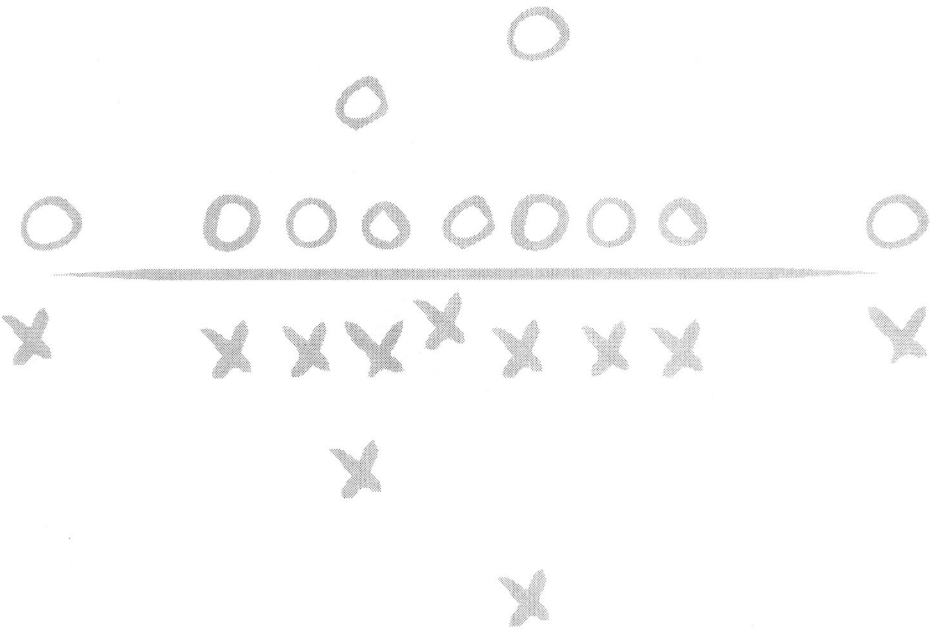

Chapter 3

I was eager about the upcoming draft. I worked rigorously with my strength coach, Keith Comeforo, that year on speed, and physical and mental attributes. NFL scouts were coming from all over to the island of Maui to watch potential draft picks to play in the Hula Bowl. I was fortunate enough to be chosen to partake. They would watch us play and practice. This was our time to show what we were made of. I was very anxious to show what I could do against top competition on a big showcase scene! Our offensive line coach was Jack Harbaugh, the father of Jon and Jim Harbaugh, our head coach was Mack Brown of the University of Texas and our main game was on a Saturday.

By then most of the scouts had already gone home because they could still watch the game on ESPN 2, however, I was ready to show what I could do and that I wanted a spot on a roster with the NFL. I felt I had a lot to prove to bullies, friends, teammates, family members and most importantly myself, that little chubby boy from middle school, because I knew what I was capable of. I had an amazing game and increased my draft status greatly with my performance in the Hula Bowl. The draft didn't start until late April, but until then I continued to practice and kept myself from being a nervous wreck during the waiting game. At that time, my brother, Jonathan, was in Las Vegas and was probably as nervous as I was. He was anxious. He understood exactly how I was feeling and the hard work I'd been doing to get what I wanted; I think he wanted it for me just as bad as I did. Jonathan had made it. He was living his dream. However, he's an older brother, protective of me and wanted nothing but great things for me. He wanted me to achieve all the best things in life like he was able to. He would call often to make sure I was focusing on the right practices and techniques. There was a lot of pressure and no downtime by this point. It was all work.

When the draft started, not one college player was ever sure if they were going to be drafted unless they were in the top 20 picks. Even if you were on the board, a scout could be looking for a quarterback when you are the world's best tackle. It was pretty frustrating.

The night before the draft I asked my father what his thoughts were and he said, "Marques, I think you're going to be a third round draft pick. I don't have a crystal ball, so right now I don't know." It was just my brother's friend and teammate and me at Jonathan's house on the first day. My nerves were shot and I was sweating bullets knowing this was going to impact the rest of my life. This was my future. Though I visited NFL franchises, scouts did come and watch me practice personally, like Jim Hanifan who was a Hall of Fame offensive line coach. He was coaching for the St. Louis Rams and had me go through a drill called push/ pull and thought I played well. There were a bunch of people who flew me out to see them, but there was still no official word, so you never really know where you stand but this was the time where all your practice mattered. After going through the 3rd round and talking to the Texans, Colts, Rams, and the Bengals I still wasn't picked. My father said, "I told you, you're good enough to be a third round pick, but it doesn't mean that you are going to be a third round pick son. This is what you go to school and fight for." I'm not sure if he was starting to get nervous for me by this time, but I then realized that I had prepared myself for so much with football except the idea of not playing football. I started to get discouraged and wasn't sleeping well. Everything was heavy on my chest, especially the thought that I wasn't going to get drafted. I had a feeling that everything I was doing wasn't good enough. I felt maybe I had done something wrong. My brother knew what I was going through; some of his friends didn't get drafted and the whole experience was just rough. When the 5th round came along, scouts were calling but had the same lines over and over again. They would say, "You are the best player available. You are the best player for our team. You are the best player who has the best personality." And yet I wouldn't hear from them after that. It felt like I was getting dumped over and over and over again. My rejection tolerance was really starting to take a toll. However, with just one call, my hopes started to rise. I got a call from the Dallas Cowboys.

The assistant coaches had seen my films, saw me play at the All Star game and thought I'd be really good for their team. However, the catch was that they didn't have a pick until the 6th round. So it was back to more waiting. Later I would find this humorous but at the time I was so mad; why would they call if they weren't ready for me?

Shortly after, I ended up getting calls from Marvin Lewis and Jack Del Rio who had both known me since I was 15. Marvin knew me because my brother played for him for the Ravens and wanted to take me on as a center. I knew Coach Del Rio back from when he coached for the Ravens in the 2000 season. My brother and that team took the Ravens to the 2001 Super Bowl against the New York Giants which the Ravens won. Coach Del Rio then became the head coach for the Jacksonville Jaguars. First off, Jack asked who all called me and then he said, "Tell them all to go away. We're going to draft you here and now." Then he hung up. I literally didn't care where it was or what team it was for; I was ready and excited. I didn't think he was serious until a few moments later when I turned around and looked at the TV.

At the bottom of the screen on ESPN it said, "Marques Ogden, offensive line, Howard University, drafted by Jacksonville Jaguars." In that moment all of my goals were achieved. My grandmother, mother, father, and I all just cried, we were so happy. I called my brother right away and he said, "I knew James Harris wouldn't let you down."

Little did I know, when I was on the phone with coach Del Rio, the owner, Wayne Weaver, was listening in and also wanted me to play for them. This was all in 2003, when my dreams had come true. News reporters, friends, family; everybody was calling to congratulate me. We went out with a few friends and family and had dinner that night to celebrate. The next day, I flew down to Jacksonville, Florida to meet my coaching staff and teammates. Eight of us were drafted: Bryon Leftwich, Rashean Mathis, Vince Manuwai, George Wrighster, LaBrandon Toefield, Brandon Green, David Young, Malaefou MacKenzie, and myself. We were all starting our dream as we were able to meet the staff, see the stadium, and the area. As excited as I was, I was still anxious because I knew this was not college anymore. This was a career.

This was a business now; it was a paycheck and peoples' livelihoods. There was tension between the new drafted players and the vets because the veteran players bubbles could be busted and they could be released if their preseason wasn't good. As much as we all wanted our team to win overall, we had to make sure that we each did something worth getting attention for. That being said, with everyone on the chopping block, we felt we were basically thrown into the lion's den. Rookies had a camp to see what it was like to play with guys who had the most talent. We played against one another and played tough because it wasn't like college. They didn't care where you came from, only what you could do to help the team. But at the same time, it was like college where vets would mentally and physically haze you. There was no malicious style hazing; it was a fun and joking style. I had my eyebrows cut off, carried several veterans' pads throughout training camp and experienced other fun style hazing. Coach Del Rio played for the Vikings, and was a kick-ass linebacker so he knew what it was like and was an advocate of rookies paying their dues. To him, it built character and strength. As rookies, we had several things to learn and respecting your veterans and teammates was just one aspect.

One thing every drafted rookie had to do was go to a symposium of three days of learning seminars, the symposium was held that year in West Palm Beach, Florida. Each one was like a group therapy with us talking about what our lives were going to be like now with fame, notoriety, money, the way girls would be chasing us, and how people would want you for all the wrong reasons. I loved it and even had Peyton Manning as a speaker as well.

Out of all the lessons we learned, the most impactful was from this beautiful woman who just walked around the hotel. Though I tried to keep my mind focused on the seminars and was still quite shy with the ladies, all of the other guys were gawking and hitting on her. She seemed very use to the attention and flirted, and made a lot of the guys feel good about themselves. One seminar was about things not being what they appear and little did everyone know, she was brought into the rookie symposium to show how one bad choice for a night can change your whole career. She was infected with the HIV virus so even though she was a beautiful woman, being with her in certain aspects could physically not only alter your playing career but your life.

They did this to help us keep focused on what we came here for and also used it as a lesson in that not everything that looks good is good for you.

Needless to say, everyone who was trying to hit on her had a gut wrenching moment where they realized they needed to prioritize their NFL career. As for me, I was scared and became even shyer with the ladies for a little while, and focused more on my NFL opportunity.

Chapter 4

"Look guys, I just want to be perfectly honest with you. It's going to be the most intense experience of your life. You're going to have to come in here and prove that you belong in this league and on this team," Coach Del Rio said in our locker room. With the first training camp we had, there were so many emotions and I felt extremely nervous. I had gotten an apartment 15 minutes away from the stadium, opposed to the some of the other players that lived in hotel rooms. My goal was to get embedded into the Jacksonville community and impress the coaching staff and personnel. My brother had told me that the best way to do that was to be at the stadium working and practicing when you didn't have to be.

On the first day of practice we weren't in pads. We moved around a lot in our positions so that the coaches could see what we were made of to see if we were tough enough to make it. I was moved to left tackle going up against Hugh Douglas whom was in his 15th or 16th season. This position was very aggressive on you, and you had to really play and be nasty.

Once I got into my zone and got used to the routines, it was a totally different experience than playing in an Organized Team Activity. In Organized Team Activities, you just played with emotions. I was pretty nervous playing with guys that I'd watch on Sundays; it was so surreal. I watched my brother on TV but he was always just my older brother who played video games with me, dared me to do stupid stuff and joked around. I always was super comfortable with him regardless of whether or not he was on TV, but for some reason, I was pretty nervous and had a hard time realizing this was my life now as well. Marco Coleman who had played one of the Dolphins players in the movie Ace Ventura Pet Detective straight up told me, "If we can sense your fear, or if we can sense that you are scared, you're a dead man.

We can look into your eyes and see if you are petrified. And you're going to understand to never show your fear if you have any ounce of it on the field. Think of it this way, the man in front of you is just a man, so play the best that you can play." That was such a true statement. When playing in any sport, the moment you show your fear, you may as well give your opponent the trophy. I learned how to hide my emotions so well, I became a pretty good poker player in the offseason.

The NFL was a business and nothing came easy. To make it, you had to earn it. They didn't care who you were, where you were from, or whose younger brother you were; only that you were there to take players' jobs because eight of them or more wouldn't be on the team like they were the previous season. It was very cutthroat. So I got beat a lot and had to learn how to play like we practiced. The first practice really set my career. Based on what the coaches said, I was being proactive opposed to being reactive. I knew I had better get ready pretty fast because my first game in the National Football League was rounding the corner.

Chapter 5

Our first game of the season was at Minnesota which was a whole surreal experience. Getting off the plane, police escorted us to the hotel where fans were waiting to see us, to see us play. We all went to dinner, slept, and then went to the stadium the next morning. Fans of both sides were going nuts and tried to get to the bus, fans of the opposing team doing so to heckle us. I had been to so many NFL games by this time and watched my brother deal with this but for the first time, I was living it and living it was exhilarating and nerve wracking at the same time. It was crazy and so different than practice; all the fans cared about was winning and their team looking good. We were just in the way.

I was full of anxiety so to calm down, I listened to classical and or instrumental music, while everyone else listened to rap to pump themselves up. I was already too pumped up. I needed to relax and live in this moment. I looked around and had one of those moments in life where you stop and live in the experience of what you are taking part in. This was it; this is what I worked hard for, what I wanted so badly and now it was here, and I was petrified. At that time, Minnesota was one of the best teams and I was going out on the field to be a gladiator and be judged; there were so many expectations as Jonathan Ogden's little brother. I told myself it was okay to have fear. Fear meant you are alive but I had to suck it up and work. Coming out of the tunnel, the Viking's mascot came out on a motorcycle so loud along with the screaming fans. He'd point his axe and shield at us acting like he wanted to cut us. My first thought was "What in the hell am I doing here? Am I ready for this?"

Once I knew I was prepared to play as a professional, the fear was gone. I went up against a guy named Kevin who was a first round draft pick from that year. Going the wrong way on my first time out, I hit him in the mouth. On the next play, he got around me late but didn't make it to the quarterback so it was basically a tie for both of us.

Needless to say, we lost the game but I was still able to get that first game under my belt and meet and mingle with the team afterwards.

Flying back, it was like leaving a part of you behind on the field. I asked the coach how I did and he said, "Not too bad, but until we see the film we won't know." The film he spoke of was what they saw on the field and even my brother said, "You can't evaluate anything until you see the film. And even then you will be told both bad things and good things as well. Coaches mostly want to push you to strive for perfection. The greatest of coaches know how to mix the good and the bad." Watching the film the next day, I learned how to critique and study my performance in a game on film in a way that pertains to real life. You had to be honest with yourself and listen to people, especially the coaches. You are there to listen to what they have to say. They don't want you to talk unless you are asked a question. Rookies seem to make that mistake of talking too much, and I definitely have the gift of gab so this was something I was afraid to mess up on and just start talking a lot. The film was very encouraging. I felt I had room for improvement but was young enough in my career to fix the problems and move on.

If you are young and coming into the NFL, you need to keep a ferocious attitude. Every day I was in the stadium learning and getting more physical on the field. I went out with veteran players to get pointers. I found the camaraderie and brotherhood in the NFL to be so much more fulfilling than I had imagined. I was creating a business but also a vast array of colleagues and companions that knew exactly what I was going through. I felt so much appreciation for the vets that were helping me build my strength, game play and overall business plan with each move and practice. Some vets may not want rookies around much, but the veterans I conversed with would often say, "My job is to pass down knowledge to you so that if you become a vet, you can pass the said knowledge down to younger kids yourself." I still feel this is part of my job even now, out of the league is mentoring the youth. I have the opportunity to pass knowledge to new players that are hungry for information to better themselves for whatever life may bring. Some very important work ethics would be to work hard, don't be late, don't call out of work, and make every opportunity a stepping-stone to the next goal.

Unless you couldn't walk, you'd better show up to practice, sick or not sick, rain or shine. Practice was where it mattered and where you were watched because that was where you were coming to work. But if you were lazy and complained, they couldn't count on you. Rookies have to earn their place on the field unlike the vets who have been there for years. I wasn't use to how practices were and practices were how we were graded and evaluated. This is your stage and you need to compete to get noticed. The cuts hadn't happened just yet, so it only persuaded us to work harder. No one is really ever prepared for the first round of cuts.

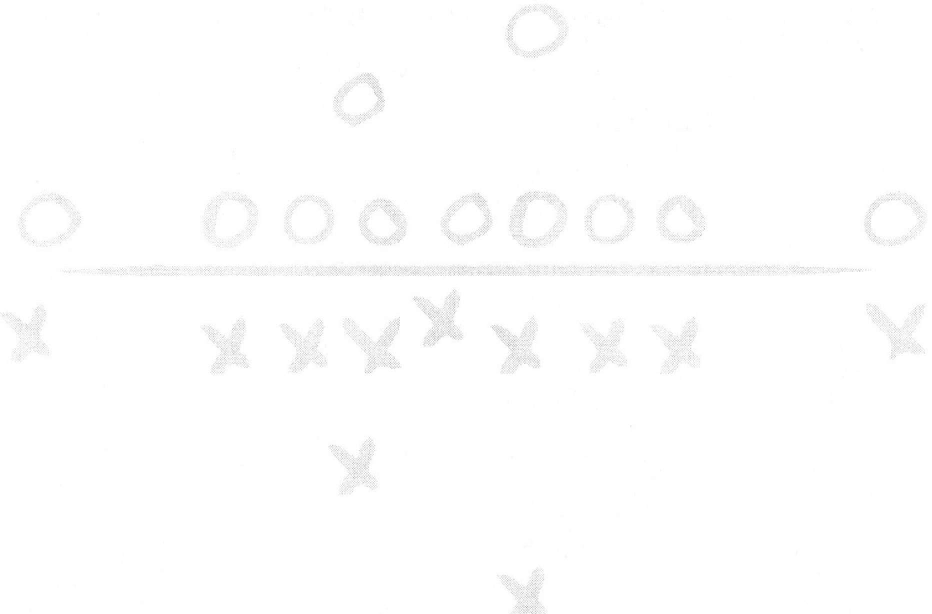

Chapter 6

On our off days, they wanted us to unwind so our minds and body had time to rest and become mentally and physically strong. I remember I spent my days watching action movies with Arnold Schwarzenegger and Jean Claude Van Damme, as well as playing poker. Practice and preseason is so grueling, it would always shock me how some rookies would still go out and party on off days. There was no way I was able to do that and be sharp for practice. Honestly too, as confident as I felt in college on the field, I was pretty shy off the field. I was petrified to get into trouble and since the symposium, I was pretty much looking at every attractive female with a side eye.

Movies and cards seemed like a safe way for me to spend my off days plus it helped me study for other positions. However, I had a lot of teammates at that time, and on my other teams I was a part of in my career, that lived for the nightlife. They loved living in the moment, when they were on a NFL roster and the notoriety it brought them. Money, girls and the fast life were the goals of a lot of players in the league. It wasn't a shock that most of those players were out of the league pretty fast and had several "baby mama" drama stories to follow. The groupies of the NFL are tough; they smell the new rookies like sharks smell blood in the ocean. I was so scared off from stories of my former teammates, I hardly dated anyone while I played in the league. Of course, these type of girls would basically throw themselves at you for a free dinner, bragging rights and a new handbag, congratulating those among them who was able to actually get pregnant and land a court order for child support. It was a profession of sorts. I had one friend who had made it to the league, went out and made a fool of himself with several women, two of which got pregnant, and got kicked off his team because he embarrassed the owners with his actions. That's the thing the NFL doesn't like; the craziness.

If you are going to go out there, act a fool and create a lot of outside drama, you'd better be a hell of a player for the NFL to actually put up with it. I found they will cut you in a heartbeat to not have to deal with it and boom, you're a former player at best. I had worked too hard, and was shy and felt awkward with this level of business to have any part of it on a serious level. I stuck to my video games and movies, and just trusted my dad when he would tell me not to bother and the right one would come along when the time was right. In the meantime, I was there for one purpose; to play football, and deposit some pretty impressive game checks. You have to learn to play every position so you can be utilized anywhere. With offensive lineman, our weapons were our hands to deliver a blow. If you were scared, you would miss and the guy would get around you, possibly running you over. I wasn't as physical as I, nor the coach, wanted me to be. You have to have the speed to play offensive tackle. The fast players playing Defensive End could be between 220 -290 lbs. The inside guys could be as heavy as 375 lbs. on the defensive line. Our team had explosive players. By week two of training camp, an offensive lineman from a Southeastern Conference school was cut from the team. This was the real deal and the NFL didn't have the patience with those who didn't put their best effort forward. It all got serious and I was trying to do the best I could just to stay there. In the second week, we were set to play Miami Dolphins in a home game.

Miami had some strong players and I went up against a defensive end from Texas named Aaron. I made a huge mistake during a protection we called 2-Jet. The running back went to the right, the offensive line would slide to the left. I ended up blocking the man in front of me, and thought everything was fine until I heard the crowd scream and roar. Turning around, our quarterback, Byron, had been sacked and fumbled the football. I remember thinking whoever messed up that play would be in big trouble. I didn't expect the coach to pull me aside and ask me what I was doing. Apparently I should've blocked the linebacker at the end of the line, which was the very guy who made the sack. Because of my mistake, the coach benched me the rest of the game. All of my studying had been thrown to the gutter, but Byron said, "Hey, it is what it is. I'm still standing."

Until this point I was a having a good game, and it being in the 3rd quarter I supported my team from the sideline. A scout pulled me aside saying, "You're playing one of the hardest positions besides the quarterback. You're going to make mistakes, but don't make the same mistake over and over again. In this game, you will win some and you will lose some. Now if you are winning more than losing, there's something there, but if you are losing more than winning you won't have a job." So many times I feel like I relive that quote, no longer with football, but with so many avenues in life. I like to think of it now as "You win some, you learn some."

After watching the film, the coach pulled me aside personally and said, "The reason I pulled you from the game is that I could see you were frustrated and I didn't want it to affect you mentally. I understand what you went through and didn't want you to cause more harm than good." At this point in my life, I definitely couldn't hide my frustrations. It probably took another ten years of my life for me to learn how to channel my frustrations to not affect the rest of my day. During the first round of cuts a week later, the personnel would walk around the stadium having each of us meet with coach Del Rio one by one with our play books. You knew if you were called in what was going on. Surprisingly enough, most of the vets were being cut and that was a big shock to me. The cuts were short and sweet and they really wouldn't tell you why due to the fact you could be playing them in a game in the near future. Although you were cut from the team, there were probably other teams who would want you. If you were to make it this far, it was something that would stick with you forever. I spent my time going about my business as normal as possible. And then by 8 o'clock that morning, if you were still in the building and attended the team meeting, you were set and made it through the first round. Going through my first cut day wasn't an easy experience. Going from a 90 man roster to 75 would only cause us to work harder in the next game against the Tampa Bay Buccaneers.

Tampa Bay was a really strong team and had some real juggernaut players. Their environment was hot and humid and I wasn't prepared to play in that sort of weather.

Being moved to right tackle, I went up against Corey Smith who was from North Carolina State and played defensive end. Corey was a super-fast player with a superb spin move. We battled against each other and I had a lot of respect for him. Sadly, he was one of four football players that went for a fishing trip and went missing. He was lost at sea. I truly felt that could have been so many of us; sometimes we feel we are big strong gladiators and invincible on the field, but then moments like this set reality in. He was a great guy and an amazing football player.

It was August when we played the game in Tampa. I grew up in DC and had some hot summers, but nothing could have prepared me for Tampa in August. I didn't train in the proper attire and became really winded. My body wasn't used to playing in that kind of environment and it exhausted me. Corey came rushing down the field and went to try and duck under me. Though I was exhausted, I tried to club him but he spun around me and got a sack. I didn't do too well that game. I was spending time with my cousin, Phyllis, and her kids watching TV after the Tampa Bay game when we saw myself on the screen.

I was so used to seeing my brother, but this time it was me. At that very moment, I got a call from James "Shack" Harris and I automatically got worried as he was telling me to be at the facility within 30 minutes. Needless to say, the whole drive there my mind was racing a million miles an hour and my heart was beating fast. I just knew this was it, I was getting cut. I walked into his office, he had me sit down and said, "I don't want to lie to you, you're playing really well right now and better than what we expected. Where we want you though, you're going to have to pick it up. I just wanted to tell you all of this personally. I've invested in you because you're a black college football player as I was, but I don't want people to think you are just here because of that. You are here because you deserve to be here. Everyone sees your talent, but they question your work ethic. Are you giving it your all? Your integrity is there, you're 100% in work outs, and you're still here."

That conversation really turned my career around. I knew I wasn't going to get cut, but it wasn't the last show. There was still work to be done. I had to ask myself, "Do I want to make the team or do I want to be put out for not giving it my all?"

Coming to work was half the battle. The rest was making your bosses and yourself happy. This was my wake up call to make football my jump start for the rest of my life. And I thank God that James Shack Harris gave me that opportunity.

The thing with James was, he knew what I was going through, but I would never understand what he had to go through to get where he was. He was the first black quarterback in the NFL and played for ten or twelve years in the '60s. He would play with teammates who'd destroy his locker and urinate in his shoes. From there, he worked his way to being a scout, then to personnel assistant, to pro personnel director in Jacksonville, and then before he retired, he became vice president of operations for the Detroit Lions. James is a great guy and said to me, "Look, I just want you to do the best you can do. If you are giving us your all, I'll take it, but I know that's not your all. I've seen you work harder and I know what you can do." He saw something in me I hadn't even discovered, but I knew I wanted to make him proud for taking the chance on me.

Chapter 7

Being older now, I realize that in life you live and learn, but back then I thought if you made a mistake, it was all over. One thing the scouts loved about me was how I'd be at the facilities working on my craft at 7 am when everyone else was supposed to be there at 8 am. I remember my brother telling me to set myself apart and show them I wanted to work hard. The one thing that matters in the NFL is your mental toughness for the game. In college ball, it becomes clear that not everybody would be great for the game. At that time playing college ball, all it took was to keep your head up and move forward. Some days were good, and then there'd be bad. It's easy to let things get to your head like money and how you spend it or if you have family in the NFL as well, and having competition with them. Hugh Douglas had once said to me, "One thing I like about you is you don't let your brother's success define who you are." This was just never an option. My brother and I are so alike in some areas and totally different in others. My dad always wanted us to be the men we chose to be. Jonathan chose to be a serious beast on the field. If I was anything like that, I'd be thrilled. However, it can be redundant answering the same questions from reporters who tried to create rivalry or quarrels, but it was never like that. We have always and continue to always support each other's ventures. I did appreciate that it was noticed from others in the game. There are a total 35 pairs of brothers who have played in the NFL at the same time. The media has often times tried to make one better than the other, one better looking than the other, one richer than the other and so on. It's ridiculous. Bottom line, these guys are family and supportive of each other. I'm not nonrealistic. I'll be the first one to say Jonathan is by far the better offensive lineman out of the two of us; he went to the Hall of Fame. Hell, he's better than most if not all who have ever put on pads for that position, and he's my brother so I love and support him, and cheer him on. The same applies the other way around. He has always been there to celebrate my triumphs and console my failures. However, while playing in the league together, it was never like we were opposing teammates. He always wanted me to do my best and be the best I was able to be. I felt as though I had proven myself enough on August 31, 2003, when Coach Del Rio had called me into his office to say, "Welcome to the 2003 Jacksonville Jaguar Roster." I immediately called my father who cried on the phone with me. I then called my brother who was proud of me and welcomed me to a whole new type of brotherhood. We didn't win very many games that year, and I did experience the realities of being a rookie as there were several instances myself and other rookies were "inducted" with our hair being cut, putting on skits for the vets, and bringing them food, especially remembering to bring it on the plane. I'm pretty sure I spent over $2500 in 17 weeks on just fast food for the vets on the team. There was one time alone at the O-Line Tight End Dinner I had to spend $5000 out of a $22,000 bill the rookies were responsible for. The veterans spared no expense ordering wine, steak, lobsters, Louis the XV alcohol; they probably ordered extra for their girlfriends at home. It was all great fun though, and when I became a veteran, I made sure to induct the rookies the same way.

Chapter 8

By the second season I was no longer a rookie, so everything with coaches and practices became easier. As a player, I wanted to do and play more on the team, but after we beat the Dolphins in our first game, I felt my line coach was having it out for me. For some reason, I was getting ripped more in evaluations and it seemed to me that he just didn't like me anymore. I never really got yelled at in high school nor at Howard, but this was putting me in a depression and at this young age, I didn't know how to handle the criticism. After talking with my brother, I knew I had two choices of either sticking it out, or have Jonathan talk to the Ravens to see if he can't get me on with them.

Being young, I was so impressionable and made the decision to leave the Jaguars so I made a call to my agent to have me switched over to the Ravens. I totally should have learned to "man-up" and deal with it. I would definitely tell my younger self to do that on many occasions.

The NFL is all a business and you have to love your franchise. Players come and go, so it's best not to get attached to them. We were expensive commodities. I should have sat down with the coaches and explained to them, like an adult, how I felt. It wasn't my line coach at all; it was me not being used to his style of coaching. All he saw was the best in me and tried to bring that out. I was being an immature kid who thought he knew how people should or shouldn't coach but every coach is different. You may have coaches that might not mesh with your personality at times and that's ok; it's a learning experience. Learn something from them and utilize their knowledge. However, I was excited to go home to Baltimore and play for the Baltimore Ravens with my brother, Jonathan Ogden. Playing for the Baltimore Ravens was a whole new experience in itself. Their fans were a class all their own and bled black and purple.

My locker wasn't far from my brother's or from Ray Lewis's. Playing alongside my brother made things a lot easier because when I played with the Jaguars, we played the Ravens so our family there couldn't choose who to cheer for. Someone had to win, and someone had to lose; it was a battle and we all understood that but celebrating after a game between our two teams was difficult for my family, so they were ecstatic we were on the same team.

It was a good year with the Ravens nonetheless, despite a scuffle I had in practice with a player named Ed who later had a stint on a Bravo reality TV show. All Ed did was test me and kept pushing me as I went back to the huddle. I thought he just didn't like me. I let it go, but then once he did it again a few plays later, I went off on him. I was a young hothead and mad. My brother being 6'9" never messed with anyone unless he was messed with first, which no one was stupid enough to do, however, he joined in on the scuffle to protect me, rightfully so this time. It not only shocked me, but it shocked the rest of the team as well. They had never seen that from him before. Bottom line, I was his little brother and he could pick on me, but wasn't a fan of others doing it.

I can say though that it made me feel good to have Jonathan stand up for me because it showed that even though we were in the NFL, we could still be brothers. Still, all Ed wanted to do was test my heart for the team to see if I was ready to play. I totally respect his point of view now and would probably do the same. You have to have heart to play the game and to be a Raven with Ray Lewis.

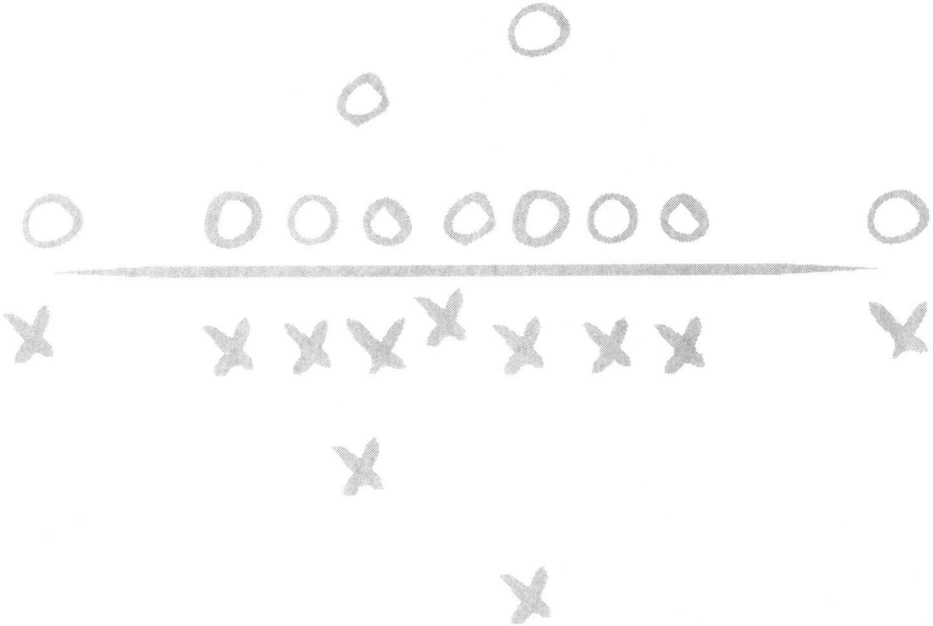

Chapter 9

The experience to meet and play for a guy like Ray Lewis was breathtaking. Ray Lewis played the game of football like the great legends from the old days; guys like Dick Butkus or Deacon Jones. He played the game like a true warrior that did not accept losing and to play alongside him was an honor. He was the team's heartbeat and could get a team pumped up like no one else. Though our season wasn't a phenomenal one, I had never been around such great fans before who supported us through winnings and losings. And the coaches were really great guys. In 2004, the Ravens opened up a new facility called the Castle where I'd spend a lot of my time in the off season practicing.

At first I lived with Jonathan and his wife until I got my own apartment. But then things started to change. Several new coaches were brought in. Everything was going well, but at the same time something didn't feel right and I couldn't put my finger on it. After talking to the coaching staff about it, I felt it was in my best interest to move on though it was disappointing to both our fans and my brother. But the Ravens and I felt I wasn't fit for their team. I wasn't sure where I was going or what my next move was, however, I had my brother and my father to lean on as my rocks for the next couple of weeks while I figured it out. My agent called and said the Buffalo Bills wanted to sign me. I'd be playing for Jim McNally a.k.a. Mouse, who was one of the best line coaches in NFL history and a small guy that knew his techniques better than anyone else. Mike Malarkey was the head coach and I did really well with the team. The Buffalo facility was close to Canada in a little blue-collar town. It was so much different than playing for Baltimore. It was so much colder and games would be played in 10 degrees below. We won possibly two or three games that season. I played alongside some great athletes, and our team had a lot of great match-ups like the Patriots in their prime.

I'm sure our lack of a winning record played a role in Coach Malarkey being fired going into my fifth year. Dick Jauron from the Chicago Bears was brought in as our new head coach, and he was awesome. I also got to play under a great director of pro personnel, Mr. John Guy, who still to this day I speak to regularly. He is a great man, and was a great front office mind. One of the good things about playing for the Bills was that some of my dad's side of the family lived close by so I was able to see them more often. When my uncle passed away from stomach cancer, I was able to get off practice to attend the funeral. My father and his girlfriend flew out and after having not seen my dad in months, I saw his health had gone down fast; his teeth decayed, and he started to have to wear dentures. He lost so much weight that he was frail. The sight of him kind of started making me very aware of his health issues. I felt like I didn't care about the NFL anymore and just wanted to be home with him as long as I could be. He didn't necessarily want this for me, but that played a huge role in why I was becoming ready to leave the NFL and return home. My dad was the type of guy that had friends everywhere he went. He always made people feel good when he was around and never had an attitude

of being better than anyone. He was definitely a
humble man. My dad had gone to the doctor for a
checkup only to find that he was suffering from
constrictive pericarditis where the valves and arteries
around the heart tighten and close off the flow of
blood to the heart. The doctors suggested an open
heart surgery, and even though I had to sign off for
it, I didn't think it was such a good idea. Dad wanted
to do it though. The surgery went just fine, and he
was put in intensive care for recovery. For three days
he couldn't speak, but was recovering. When he did
speak on the third day, he said, "Marques, I love you,
but get out. I have to sleep." I really didn't want to
leave, but I gave in and said, "Bye, I love you too.
I'll see you later."

Two o'clock in the morning the very next day on July
26th 2006, I got a phone call from the hospital
saying my father was having complications. Driving
90 miles an hour, I got there at 3:28 and had to wait
in the waiting room. A doctor soon came in to say
that my father had died at 3:21, just 7 minutes before
I got there. The hardest calls I had to make in my life
ever were to my mom and brother. My mother had
let out a gut wrenching scream and immediately hung
up the phone to drive there.

He had died of asphyxiation, choking on his own vomit. I felt so bad for him to be spending his last minutes of life that way to no one else's fault. My mother went in at the same time with me and he was like a ghost, pale and so still. I never expected to see him that way.

Thousands of people attended his funeral. He had so many friends and it was a super packed house. Most of the Ravens team was there and brought busloads of people along with them. I held it together as much as I could until we were putting him in a mausoleum. That's when it hit me that he was gone. I cried for five minutes straight, and my brother had to pick me up and hold me because I was going through so much grief. It was unreal that I lost my best friend. I still needed my dad; I still feel like I need my dad. It wasn't fair. My dad had just turned 57 and it was the darkest time of my life. Both Jonathan and I contemplated on retiring from football all together. We both took time off, and I became depressed and started drinking profusely. I just didn't want to live anymore.

Chapter 10

2007 was a blur to me. Losing someone who raised you so unexpectedly is a really tough situation to deal with. I stayed out most nights drinking, gambling, and living life in a way I shouldn't have. I was drinking a whole fifth bottle of Hendricks gin mixed in with tonic every night for about six months straight! I would drink at home by myself, or I would go out to the bar with my friends, and drink to excess. Those same friends who protected me from trouble before I got drafted would keep an eye on me so I wouldn't hurt myself or put myself in a position to hurt others. I was beside myself with grief. I would be gambling thousands of dollars at the darkest, dirtiest poker halls in East Baltimore city not far from Interstate 95.

I would literally play poker for 24-36 hours straight or as long as I could keep my eyes open at the gambling table. I just couldn't cope with my father, the one I depended on in life, the one who got me to all my success, talked me thru my problems was no longer there. At the end of the day, I was still going through so much pain and turmoil that I truly didn't want to live anymore. I thank the Lord for sending angels to protect me in those dark moments. I remember I used to play poker at a house at least 3-4 times a week. I didn't care if I won or lost; I just needed the mind numbing game to get me through the night. There was one night I was on my way to a house and got a call that I had to take care of something for my dad's estate. I was unable to make it to the house game that night. I found out the next morning that the game had been interrupted by three masked gunman with shotguns who robbed the house and injured all who were there. I knew my dad was looking out for me, even from beyond.

I started to spend more time on the golf course to help come out of my stage a bit, and then decided on not renewing my contract with the Bills in the off season. I didn't practice with anybody, and being financially stable from playing well enough before-hand, I waited to see what would happen next. I loved Buffalo but I had too many memories of my dad being there, cheering me on in the stands that I felt in order for me to move on, I needed to physically move on.

Gambling one night I got a call from my agent that the Tennessee Titans wanted to bring me into Nashville and see what I could do. My first thought was "Hey, it's the South and could be a good chance to get away." I was put in a hotel and worked out with the team running drills. They knew of my drinking problem, but wanted to see if I could leave that all behind. Within three days they wanted to sign me. Like I said, each coach you have will be different in how they coach you. My head coach with the Titans was Jeff Fisher, a man I was fortunate to play for. Things were starting to look up. I didn't work out in the off season though and because I wasn't taking care of myself from drinking and staying up all night, it all took a toll on my body. I became a mere shadow of myself. We played our first game against the Redskins and my back completely locked up at the end.

I couldn't recharge my body, so after the third game I knew I couldn't go forward and told my coach all of what was going on. I ended up getting a settlement with my back and leaving the NFL. I know my father was probably looking down from Heaven and not wanting me to leave, but my mental and physical shape wasn't prepared. I had so much grief to deal with and felt very alone. I should have put all my effort in the game but I was putting it all into self-destruction. I didn't know where I belonged anymore. Before my father passed away, I bought us a house in Baltimore so that I could take care of him when he was out of the hospital. He had sold our childhood home and when I came home from Nashville, I still had to get all of his things together and settle his personal affairs. My mother struggled as well because they were still pretty close and I believed my father still loved her until the day that he died. Even though he was going to get married to his girlfriend, he knew being sick he couldn't provide for her, so he just gave up and let it all go.

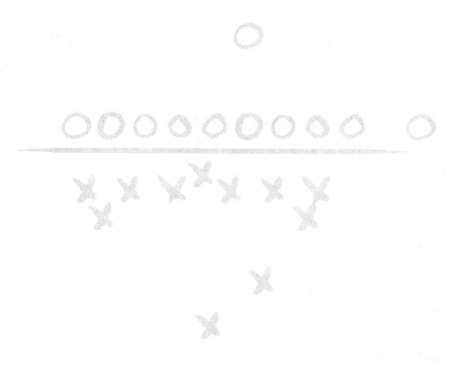

Chapter 11

I realized I had to get off my butt and move forward because if I didn't, I would end up exactly like him. I would die at a young age with nothing show for it. Something had to give. I had a little bit of experience with business because of classes I took in college, so I met up with a colleague looking for a partner in real estate, along with a third party associate. Due to my mom's request, we got with a lawyer and had background checks done on all of us. Though my colleague and I came up clean, the third party had thirteen cases of fraud and embezzlement. So we decided it wasn't a good idea going into business with him. This was a warning sign and reminded me of my rookie year symposium with the lady with HIV. Things and people aren't always as they seem. My colleague and I started up Kayden Premier Enterprises named after my brother's kid's name and opened up a small office in downtown Baltimore. I had invested a huge chunk of my own personal money, and had my name and face on this company. I had gone to a convention for minority contractors in Baltimore and met Congressman Elijah Cummings who was very well respected. We got to talking and he said that the first five years of starting a business are the hardest, but once you get past that, you will know if you will succeed. Keeping his advice in mind, my uncle set us up with a meeting with someone who was known as the "King of Minority Construction" in Baltimore County that did site work and utilities. Starting out, I used my NFL personality to make contacts and get us started with small work in demolition and concrete. Jobs were coming in at $5,000 and we'd get paid in 30 days.

Working both in Maryland County and Baltimore City, jobs were starting to pick up. Closing out the first year we brought in $75,000 and rarely worked out of the office. By year two, jobs were paying half a million dollars which brought in enough money for us to be able to bring on a full time crew.

Often times, there were problems at sites, but the jobs still got completed and we stayed in the small office. We didn't have anything to show stability just yet for a bank loan, but money was still good. I guess at this time, I let my guard down. I wasn't in the NFL anymore where I felt people would circle like vultures to get a piece of you, but I had no idea the type of people who would be circling afterwards to take advantage of you. We felt like we weren't going anywhere in the business so I started to question my partner's work habits in running operations, but never really looked into it. I still trusted him at the time. Don't get me wrong, I think he was able to manage some small jobs, but sometimes when your company is going to go to the next level, not everyone is suited to take that step.

Year three, we brought on a bigger staff to work with bigger projects. This was probably the beginning of the end. I would suggest to small companies that just because you are growing, doesn't mean you need to hire a ton of people all at once, but we were excited that we were growing and thought this was what we were supposed to do. We got the Shining Star Award which is the up and coming award for young companies that are accomplishing big projects and jobs, and show they are on their way to success and prosperity, given out by Mr. Paul Taylor and the Small Business Resource Center. We were also finally certified as a minority contractor in the city of Baltimore, and the state of Maryland. The work started coming to us instead of us chasing work. We grossed 4 to 5 million dollars in revenue that year. Things seemed to be going well, but I wasn't paying any attention to the bottom line. When year four came around, we brought in 8 to 10 million. Being so young and inexperienced, I started noticing our mistakes. Invoices to clients were being turned in late, or they were being under billed and not notarized. Our financial books weren't in order and the field staff was either not showing up at all or showing up drunk on the sites. Trusting we could get out of it, we brought in 11 to 12 million dollars in year five but then things started going downhill fast. I felt like I no longer had control. There were a ton of people working in the office, the payroll got huge and the due diligence wasn't always done to the point of not even doing reference checks on people working for MY company. I take responsibility for this because I either chose to partner with or chose to hire the people that were supposed to make sure we had the right people in line. It was becoming a mad house at the office. I was so young and inexperienced, and still learning how to be a businessman. I thought that meant to throw your weight around and show who's in charge. That was definitely not the way to work. There was a lack of respect, and a lack of professionalism and maturity in our work environment, from myself included. This was not the way to build a company and I felt we were soon becoming a laughing stock. Companies that hired us to work also noticed this. I would get calls around the clock about my workers, my partner and me only dealing with things by blowing up at people or drinking. I felt I had no one to turn to in a way. Things were rough. I was "friends" with people in my office but I later realized I wasn't really; I was a paycheck to them and by being "friends", they could come in late, get advances on paychecks, take advantage and I just let them get away with it. I wasn't ready to be a boss and manage people. I was great at meeting with clients and getting work, but my staff and operations couldn't deliver. I over promised and under delivered, and eventually got a huge project that I was encouraged to take. Against better judgment, my operations manager assured me we could do it and I accepted. I wanted our name on this project!

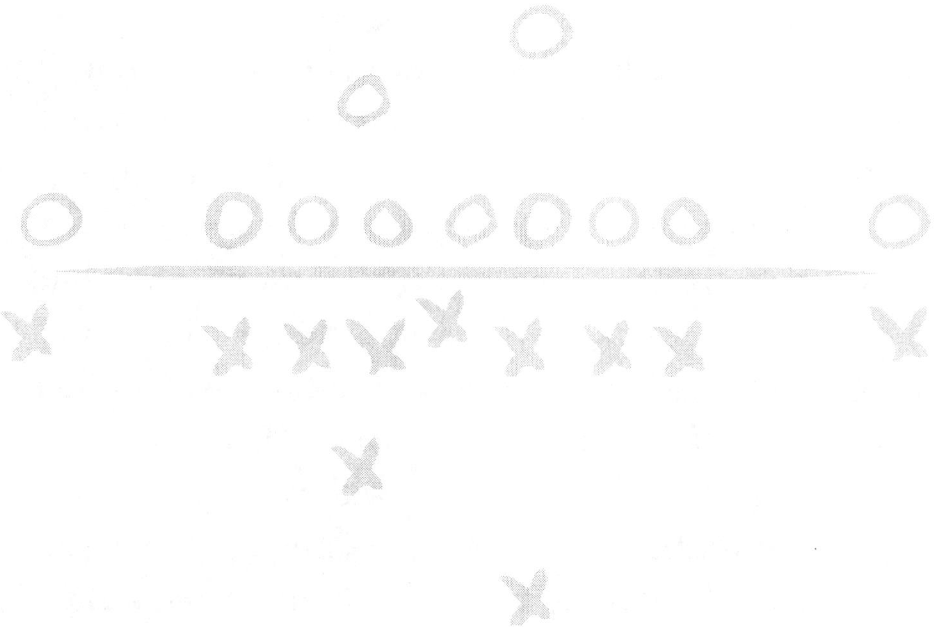

Chapter 12

In my personal life, I had always been kind of a shy guy. I was friends with a lot of people but never really chased a woman. I had dated here and there but honestly, there was never anyone that had the substance to be someone really important in my life. I was just filling time with random people. I also was insecure from leaving the NFL as a big guy, and then creating bad habits from losing my dad, so the women that I would date or be with were people that I felt comfortable with; I never aspired for better. A couple friends of mine noticed this and wanted me to kind of raise my standards, and have more of an option to meet the right person.

They had some experience with online dating and created a profile for me on Match.com. At first I thought there was no way I was going to go along with it. I had heard too many horror stories. So, I didn't really give it much thought and was still trying to figure out what was going on with my company; Match was just a monthly payment, until one day. I had my account linked to my phone, so suddenly I get this "wink" from someone from North Carolina. For one, I was like "How would this even work out?" and second, her pictures were just so gorgeous, I couldn't believe it was real. The pictures had to have been fakes. I thought for sure it was a scam. This is the type of girl I would look at from afar and admire at the club or something but NEVER even try to talk to because I would think she was out of my league, and here she is "winking" at me. I sent her a quick email and went about my business. She emailed me back and we started exchanging emails throughout the day. I still thought this woman was probably fake and that it was probably her cousin's picture or something because I wasn't used to women like her. I decided on asking her to Skype and talk on the phone just to be sure she was as cute in real life. Sure enough, it really was her and

I thought apparently North Carolina grows some attractive women. The more we talked, the more we got to know each other and in early August, I asked her to come see me in Baltimore. I didn't think anything of it. I told her I would buy her a flight and she can come hang out. Knowing her now, she probably thought about this decision for a long time and it probably made her super uncomfortable. She watches a lot of Dateline and 48 Hours and was worried about meeting some stranger out of her comfort zone. She did decide to come though. I remember picking Bonnie up from the airport in my Hummer. She was walking to the car with her skinny jeans and leather jacket, big purse and long blonde hair. I was like "Thank You God!!!" Being a shy guy with no "player" mentality, I didn't really put much effort into what I wore to meet her and showed up in sweat pants and a black tee. She still rips on me for showing up to meet her for the first time in sweat pants. I am pretty sure she has thrown those sweat pants in the trash since. I later found out she brought Mace in her purse, just in case I got out of hand. I had no idea I could have been maced that weekend. She was definitely different.

There was a maturity about her and I knew me having formerly been in the NFL was not something she was remotely interested in, in fact, it may have worked against me. She was so incomparable to the type of girls I was used to. She even had my pit bull house trained and taught him how to give kisses the first day she met him.

That short weekend was amazing and I found myself finding reasons to go to North Carolina to see her. The first time I met her family I was helping her move into a new house. I remember thinking how awesome her big family was and how nice and welcoming her parents were. I had previously dated people whose families had issues with multiracial dating, so I was a little uptight about how things would go. I was also a little terrified since her dad was a minister and I felt some apprehension since I hadn't been in church since my dad's passing. Her family was so accepting and loving though. From her parents to siblings to nieces and nephews, they treated me with such compassion and were so gracious to get to know me. Her family values were so like those of my dad and grandparents. It was comforting to me getting to know them as Bonnie and I became serious almost overnight.

We would usually alternate weekends; I would go there one weekend, and she would come to Baltimore the next. Being young and in love suddenly, we were ready to be together all the time. She quit her job as a teacher and moved to Baltimore with her eight year old daughter, Ava, a few months after we met. Things were going real well with my personal life, but business wise, not so much.

Chapter 13

Kayden had become one of the largest minority contractors in the city of Baltimore, and the state of Maryland. We did a lot of work at John Hopkins Hospital and were awarded a project for DHMH Health Laboratory. Working with the owner we completed the first task of demolishing the asphalt and parking lot. Then we began excavating the dirt. With the project being a 4 million dollar one, we thought we were on top of the world. Things were coming along smoothly, but we were so focused on the job, other projects weren't getting done. Jobs weren't being bid properly and we were losing money along with owing money to people. Being behind a month on ten jobs is ten months of labor that has to be paid back. Things from years three and four had caught up with me in my fifth year. Dead assets were causing issues for us trying to get an extra line of credit. And to make matters worse, I didn't do background checks or even check applications of the new employees I had hired and found out they didn't have the experience they once said they did. Suppliers weren't working with us and weren't letting us buy supplies because of late payments. Bills just piled up.

Kayden's weekly payroll was $50k a week, but still wasn't enough to complete the contract work on the project. I had to cash stock investments, and had over time borrowed close to half a million dollars. Now I started to get worried because I had just moved in with my girlfriend, and had so much pressure on my chest. There were so many issues that all started caving in professionally which made it difficult for me to enjoy my new personal life. The phone calls about problems at the sites poured in, no money was coming in and more bills had to be paid. I didn't want to let anyone down and was searching for solutions. I had a couple investors that were going to take part ownership in the company, however, it went from a problem to a panic mode real fast and I was shocked when clients were telling me I would be closed down within six months if I didn't find a way to fix things as soon as possible. I put all my own personal money in this company. I was set to lose everything if this didn't work. I was doing all I could to get people paid on time that I would often not pay myself; I fell behind on my mortgage and maxed out my credit cards. I remember giving Bonnie my credit card to go to the grocery store to get food for the week. She called me from the car yelling at me as she was humiliated. She apparently had been ready to check out at the grocery store and had all the food on the belt, but my card wouldn't work. Here is a woman that left her job, her family, her home and put her trust in me and I couldn't even pay for groceries? I would sit up at night wondering what I was going to do. I was about to lose it all as well as my girlfriend. Why did I convince her to quit her job and move here when I can't even provide? I didn't want to tell her how stressed I was and what was happening. Bonnie is a smart lady and knew something was up though. She did her own due diligence and found out what was going on with my business. She started noticing people for who they were in my life so people I worked with felt threatened by her.

They were able to play their "friendships" over my head but she has a way of seeing through people. Let's just say, the beautiful lady at the Rookie Symposium wouldn't have fooled her. She knew it was something I needed to see on my own though. She never came out and told me how she felt about certain people for a while. However, it was clear people were also seeing her and that she was real and had my back. I suddenly started having people from work tell me how bad she was for me. It was quite convenient for them to not approve as she was unraveling their lies.

It's only natural in cases like this that you want to blame someone for failure. Bottom line, it was my own fault. This was my company, my money I lost, my name on it and my face representing it. I should have been more careful with who I partnered with, who I hired, and what jobs I accepted. I should never have invested all of my own money. However, regardless of this, it was getting out of control. I had people threatening me legally and physically. These were people I helped out, people I went to court for, gave money to, even bought their kids' diapers for in bad times, and all they wanted to do was see me suffer.

I was completely shocked. I now have a woman and an eight year old little girl living with me and people want to hurt me? I couldn't sleep; I didn't sleep. I was so stressed out and had no idea of what to do, all the while, bleeding money from my personal account. As scared as I was to lose Bonnie, she rolled up her sleeves and let me know she was ready to work. I knew my dad had led me to her. He found someone who had no problem calling out the fake people in my life and getting in line to fight them off with me. Many people would say, "Just go to your brother and ask him for help to save the company." I remember Bonnie saying, "NO!!! This is your mess, YOU are going to fix it and learn from it!" It was time to grow up.

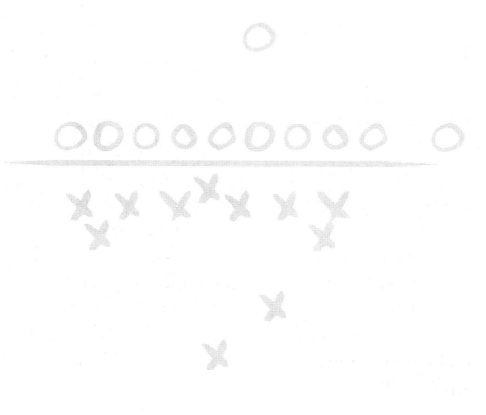

Chapter 14

I knew Kayden was done. I wasn't the typical NFL guy who blew his money on cars, jewelry, women, and expensive homes. I used every dime I had from my NFL savings and from what my father had left from selling off his house to help save Kayden but it wasn't enough. I went from being a millionaire to having less than four grand in the bank basically overnight in the grueling world of construction and big corporate America business. I lost almost 2 million dollars in just under 90 days. When you lose that much money in such a short amount of time, it really takes a toll on you mentally, physically and emotionally all at the same time!

Can you just imagine working your whole life to play for the NFL, start a business that you could see your future in, and then go from making eight figures to closing the doors in less than 90 days right at the beginning of your sixth year? It's heartbreaking. I wasn't a bad guy; I just made a bad choice in taking on a project that I wasn't properly funded to handle. I saw huge dollar signs, and took my eye off the prize of running the company objectively and professionally!

People would be stealing stuff from the office; trucks, computers. It was just total chaos and mutiny. Cleaning out my office drawer, I found my NFL player card, called the office telling them how much trouble I was in, and asked for help. The NFL got to work right away to shop my resume out to potential employers. The NFL office signed me up for the Gene Upshaw Trust Fund Program for players who need help. The way it works is when NFL players get fined in games, the league takes that money that is collected, puts it into a program, and then it goes out to players who are in financial need. The Gene Upshaw Trust Fund Program was created to be a financial bridge for players that are in dire financial needs.

Programs like these are rarely publicized by the media; they are there to help former players who are willing to help themselves and learn from their mistakes. They help people find gainful employment, credit counseling, emotional and mental counseling, short term financial relief and many other resources.

After I scraped up all the documents I needed, the NFL got me a job interview with Merrill Lynch at the Durham, North Carolina office. In the meanwhile, we looked for a small house in North Carolina, as it was time to close the doors to Kayden and start a new chapter. We moved in April of 2013, and after paying the movers and rent, we had $2100 in the bank. The stress mounted, but Bonnie who was now my fiancé, was still there when I felt no one else was. I thank God for her strength and love everyday as we lost cars, homes, and pretty much everything we owned which can cause stress in any relationship. We worked through all of the struggles and came out stronger than ever at the end of the whole ordeal. One day, I remember sitting on the couch with her just venting on what all seemed to happen so fast, and had one of those moments where you realize that what you are going through at that very second will influence your life in so many ways.

She even told me, "Remember this feeling, and live in this moment. We won't be back to this after we get this cleared up." I felt like a failure. Stressed out, I started drinking again and it started to take a toll on my family life. I never slept. I would be up at all hours of the night pacing, and I would just drink and drink and drink some more! There were so many sleepless nights. I found fault with myself and Bonnie and created turmoil in our relationship. We were both young and hot heads and would often times argue and fight unfairly. We realized we needed to create a safe boundary together to be successful. However, the problems at hand continued. My phone got turned off, and the two cars we had were about to be repossessed. Bonnie got a job and found a food pantry to help us out as we tried to figure out if we'd even have enough money to pay the next month's rent. Bonnie called me one afternoon and had a certain tone in her voice that made me scared. I couldn't handle any more bad news. She quickly told me that we just got a letter in the mail, and that the NFL Gene Upshaw Trust was going to pay the next four months of rent and bills for us to get ourselves back on track. I remember I was driving and had to pull over because I was about to cry.

I needed help. I had lost everything and had a bankruptcy in process for my own personal self and the company in the near future. But here, even after I no longer played, I still was a part of a group. When I was down and overwhelmed, the NFL Player Care Foundation came and picked me up. This gave both Bonnie and myself the strength to go out and make money. I stopped working for Merrill Lynch and created my own brand of football camps. We worked hard. I started doing one on one training with football, birthday parties, camps, and appearances; there was nothing beneath me that I wouldn't do to save money and salvage my family. We managed to save about ten thousand dollars in four months and didn't slow down.

Around this time, we found out we were expecting a baby. We were both very excited and it gave me the incentive to work even harder. I was about to have another mouth to feed. This little girl would add to my motivation as a father and man. I found myself thinking about my dad at times trying to find ways to be the man that would make him proud. My daughter, Farrah Ivy Ogden, was born on my dad's birthday.

It was such a day of celebration. I was reminded of how he continues to look out for me and the beautiful gift God had given our family. She is a perfect blend of our families and inspires me to be the best man in her life. I don't have sons to teach the game to, but I have two daughters to teach the game of life to. I aspire to teach them to learn through the struggle and make it to the other side all the while knowing I will always have their back.

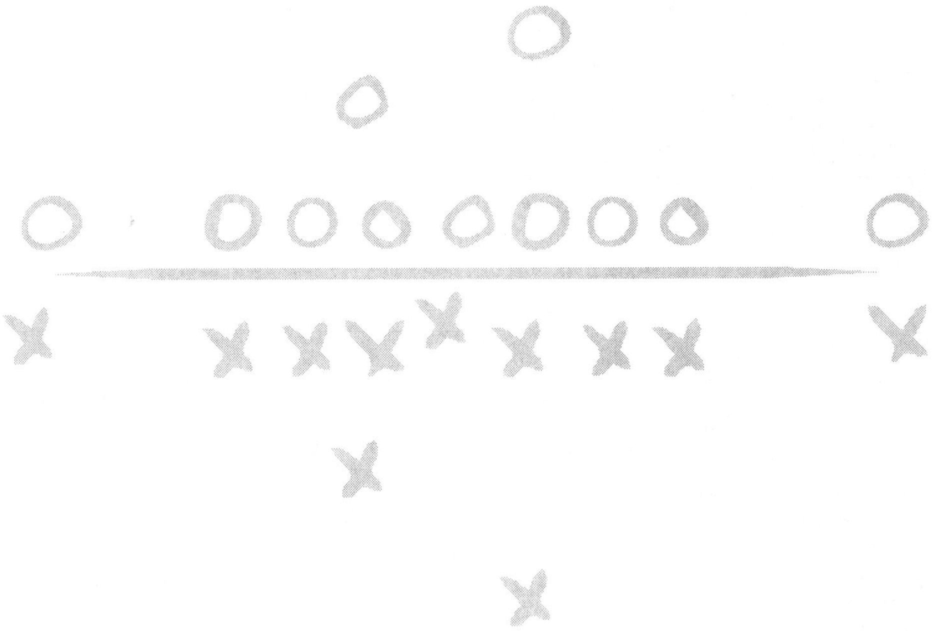

Chapter 15

I continued to grind daily. I focused on my personal growth from the man I was to the man I was to become. I remembered when I wanted to quit football and my dad told me to "Go out there and show them what you're made of, and earn your spot." I needed to earn my spot in life. I was going to show myself I could be successful off the field as well. I surrounded myself with good people who didn't "need" things from me. I got linked up with a great team of people to have involved in my brand. I went from having it all and being on TV every weekend to losing everything I worked hard for but I was still going and still ambitious to have the rest of my life be the best of my life.

At this point, I'm on the build. I work closely with many programs to help other athletes to not make the same mistakes that I did and talk to youth on a daily basis as a mentor. I find myself trying to be a pioneer like my grandfather to keep young men off the streets and make the right decisions in life.

I talk to corporate companies as a public speaker about the issues that I faced in my downfall and how to prevent that from happening to them. I have learned so much from my personal journey, and aspire to help other people with their life experiences. I have spoken for Fortune 500 Companies, Fortune 100 Companies, universities, prestigious organizations and much more! I truly love sharing certain avenues and parts of my life to help others make informed and educated decisions on what to do in their lives. I am involved with athletes' health with Gamebreaker Helmet and as a NFL Fuel Up to Play 60 spokesperson. I currently own a National Youth Football Organization 7 on 7 franchise as well as football camps.

The National Youth Football Organization holds a very special place with me as it gives youth the opportunities to learn from former NFL players as their coaches. I also am a member of many NFL Alumni groups, including the NFL Trust Program. The NFL Trust Program is a program designed to help former players connect with each other. They have business programs, and many other various partnerships, that help former players transition into their next phase of life. The Trust has been very important in helping me transition smoothly from my playing days.

I am also a spokesperson for a national recruiting company, Athlete YOUniversity. Our mission is to help get kids exposure to help them ascend to the next level of playing their sport of choice at the collegiate level. I recently got married to my wife who stuck by me through it all. I'd give this woman the world for her strength and devotion. I am the father of two beautiful daughters who motivate me daily. I started really working out, watching what I ate, going to church again, and creating hobbies to relieve stress. I lost about 105 lbs. since my NFL career. When my daughter was born, I knew that I had to change my lifestyle so I could be here for her and my eleven year old. My father died early in his life due to physical ailments and I did not want my girls to have to go through the same pain and anguish I went through by losing a father at such a young age! I have regained control of my health and lifestyle. I no longer drink very much at all and have learned to accept myself throughout each and every stage of learning in my life. I was very hesitant to tell my story to people as all the hard work I had done and dedication I had in the NFL, and in corporate America to build my future for my family and me, I felt, had failed when it all came crashing down around me and I had to file for personal bankruptcy. Opening up about my story was very difficult initially, but I was determined to not let others make the same mistakes and failures I made in my life. I decided to share my story openly with people in every essence of my brand and my everyday life, so I could really make a difference to others living.

Life is great; day-by-day I use my now renewed faith to lead by example and not by word, and I've learned how to become a man of faith and trust God out of a life of darkness. Throughout my life, God had brought me up from the worst part of things to this point where I have a positive outlook on life.

No matter what, He is always there and no matter what I went through, God brought me out of my darkest times. Through it all I have learned that despite what fumbles life throws you, you can always become something special.

Above:Ogden posing for a photo shoot when he was 27 years old

Above:Ogden and Hall of Fame Football player Mr. Lawrence Taylor
in Wake Forest NC in summer of 2015

Above: First Picture Bonnie and
Ogden ever took together in 2012

Below Right: Bonnie and Ogden at a
Who's Who Event in Baltimore City

Bottom Left: Ogden, Ava, Bonnie and Zeus taking a Christmas photo in 2012

Above: Ogden, Ava and Farrah going to church in spring of 2015

Above: Ogden teaching football to some young campers in Augusta Georgia
for Factory Athletics July of 2015

Above: Ogden and his old college OL teammates from Howard working his football camp in Holly Springs, North Carolina

Above: Bonnie and Ogden at a Smart CEO awards dinner in 2012

Below Left: Bonnie and Ogden at the Washington DC mall in 2012 first family outing

Below Right: Ava and Ogden posing in November of 2012

Above: Ogden with former NC State Basketball star Danny Strong in Fall of 2013

Above: Ogden and two time Super Bowl Champion Willie Parker working
the Holt Brothers Camp in June 2015

Above Left: Bonnie and Ogden at a wedding in Charleston SC 2012

Above: Ogden having dinner with Torry Holt, Terrance Holt, and Corey Chavous in downtown Raleigh the night before coaching the Holt Brothers Camp in June of 2015

Below: Ogden talking to kids at a lineman challenge at Apex High School in summer of 2013

Above Left: Ogden and Bonnie on their first out of state trip together to Richmond VA

Above Right: Ogden and Ava posing for a picture in NC home 2013

Below: Ogden, Ava and Zeus taking a Christmas picture in Dec 2013

Above: Ogden teaching Russell Wilson how to pass block at his Russell Wilson Passing Camp in June of 2015

Above Right: Ogden and his brother Jonathan working out at Ravens practice in summer 2006

Below: Ogden and his boy Steve LaPlanche at a Baltimore Mariners indoor football game in summer of 2011

Above: Ogden at a photo shoot in New York City for Traphic Magazine in March of 2015

Below: Ogden and his brother in the summer of 1987

Above: Ogden, his mom and brother at his charity boxing night in fall of 2011

Below: Ogden, his dad and brother at his brothers high school graduation in summer of 1992

Above: Ogden and Farrah going to watch some football in fall 2014

Above: Ogden and Farrah going to Sunday Church in spring 2015

Below: Ogden, his brother, and Steve Geppi owner of Geppis comics in summer 2011

Above: Ogden, his mom and brother in summer 1986

Above: Ogden's dad, this was taken in early 2000s. He has this exact picture tattooed on his back!

Below Left: Ogden and his brother pose for a fun magazine at an amusement park when he was 7 years old

Below Right: Ogden holding Farrah like a football in fall 2014

132

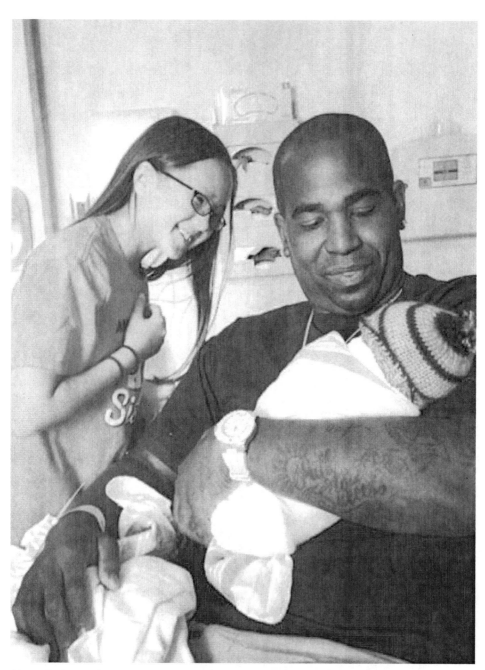

Above: Ogden, and Ava with Farrah the day she was born July 18th, 2014

Above: Ogden and Farrah going to church in spring of 2015

Below: Ogden and Ava at Bonnie's old house in summer 2012

Above: Ogden and Bonnie having a selfie moment in the summer of 2015

Below: Ogden at a photo shoot in New York City for Traphic Magazine in March 2015

Above Left: Ogden's picture with the
Tenensse Titans in fall 2007

Above Right: Ogden and Bonnie having a home
movie night in summer 2015

Below: Ogden playing Offensive line talking to his teammates in fall 2005

Above: Ogden practicing football in summer 2011

Below: Ogden, and all of the oline teammates from Howard University posing for the camera in fall 2001

138

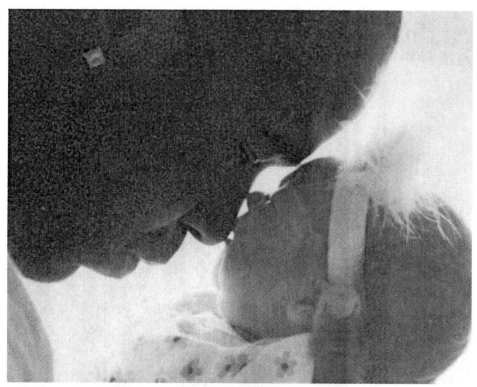

Above: Ogden's first professional picture ever with Farrah on July 20, 2014

Below Left: Ogden, Bonnie,and Ava at
Christmas Eve Service in winter 2012

Below Right: Ogden doing dumbbell incline
press in the gym in Baltimore in Summer 2011

Above: Ogden public speaking for the Boys and Girls club in Raleigh in spring 2015

Above: Ogden holding Farrah at Avas cheer competition in spring 2015

Above: Ogden, Ava and Farrah picking out a pumpkin for Halloween 2014

Above: Ogden and Bonnie at Yankee Stadium on their honeymoon in May 2015

Below Left: Ogden and Bonnie sharing a tender moment in spring 2015

Below Right: Farrah in Ogden's jersey in summer 2015 with Zeus following her

Above:Odgen and Ava at the Baltimore Zoo in fall 2012

Above: Picture of Kayden used in magazine ad in summer 2010

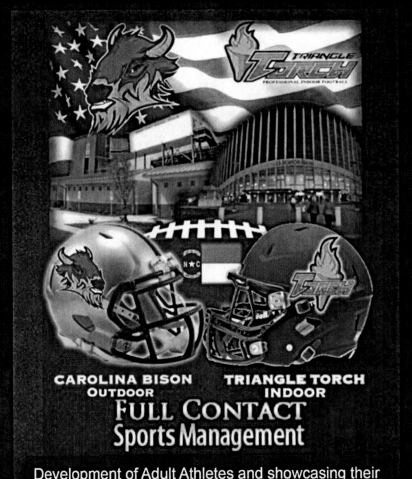

CAROLINA BISON **TRIANGLE TORCH**
OUTDOOR INDOOR

FULL CONTACT
Sports Management

Development of Adult Athletes and showcasing their talents through Professional Indoor and Outdoor Football please visit our websites www.fullcontactsportsmgmt.com & Triangletorchproindoorfootball.com Great opportunity to invest in or support our organizations which has a huge impact in the Triangle!
Contact us 919-473-6081 or toll free at 888-613-0684.
"Small Enough to Care, Large Enough to Serve"
Email haroldncbison@yahoo.com &
info@fullcontactsportsmgmt.com

GAMMS UNLIMITED
Youth and Adult Life/Career Coaching

At GAMMS UNLIMITED, there is no one size fits all approach to helping others become who they were born to be. **It's ALL ABOUT YOU** because we want you to live and enjoy life to the fullest! Once you know who you are, and you articulate and communicate your strengths, you create unlimited options and opportunities to excel. GAMMS UNLIMTED's mission is to help people work, live and build their career: One generation at a time! One person at a time, One student at a time!

GAMMS UNLIMITED relieves the pressure of helping students and professionals make critical career and education decisions by helping them make choices that reflect their talents. GAMMS UNLIMITED personalizes programs to meet youth and adults needs such as:

ASSESSMENTS	COACHING	WORKSHOPS & SEMINARS
Student	Students (Middle, High, College/Technical)	Basic Life and Interpersonal Skills
Adult	Adults in Career Transition (Unemployed, under-employed, pre and post retirement)	Career and Workplace Readiness
Lawyer	Individuals who wish to discover their natural abilities	
Leadership	Group coaching	

GAMMS UNLIMITED coaching resources help:
- Students to define their directions and plan for college
- Adults achieve greater career satisfaction
- Businesses effectively develop skills of their employee
- Promotes self-understanding
- Builds self-confidence.

GAMMS Unlimited facilitates basic skills workshops such as Team Building, Note Taking, Study Skills, Test Taking, Career Identification, and Mock Interviewing. We also share existing community resources to help actualize goals and dreams.

GAMMS UNLIMITED has worked with or been associated with large and small consulting organizations focusing on life and career coaching, performance development consulting, mentoring, and individual and group coaching such as Carrboro/Chapel Hill Blue Ribbon Mentoring, Knightdale High School – Business Alliance, Durham Technical Community College, Dallas County Community College-Richland Campus, North Carolina State University (Business Coaching Program), Jack & Jill-Capital City Chapter, National Black MBA Association, Inc. (Leaders of Tomorrow), Jobs for Life-Raleigh, North Carolina Project Management Institute, Celebration Church-NC, North American Council for Staff, Program and Development, and American Diabetes Association-Raleigh just to name a few.

GAMMS UNLIMITED, LLC
919-349-1726
gammsunlimited.com

148

NORTH CAROLINA HEART & VASCULAR

UNC HEALTH CARE

North Carolina Heart & Vascular is a cardiology practice offering comprehensive heart and vascular care. Our experienced cardiologists and staff specialize in the diagnosis, treatment and prevention of cardiovascular disease. We are members of the UNC Heart & Vascular Network and collaborate with other specialists throughout the region to make sure our patients have access to the treatment, resources and support needed for long-term health right in their communities when possible. Contact your local North Carolina Heart & Vascular office for more information, to schedule an appointment or to refer a patient.

NOW AVAILABLE
from VIP INK PUBLISHING, L.L.C.

Author — Only A Guy
Hard Questions About God
ISBN # 978-0984738205

Author — Stanley Simmons
The Great Deception: Why Are They Here?
ISBN # 978-0984738274

Author — Only A Guy
The Book Of Prayers
IBSN # 978-0984738229

Author — Only A Guy
Hard Questions About Christianity
ISBN # 978-1939670038

Author—Dr. Thomas Moore
Holy Wars: Root Causes
ISBN # 978-1939670021

Author — Only A Guy
Hard Questions About Creation
ISBN # 978-1939670069

Author — Robert Conners
They Are Real
ISBN # 978-0984738298

Author — Only A Guy
Hard Questions About The Holy Spirit
ISBN # 978-0984738236

Author — Only A Guy
Hard Questions About Jesus
IBSN # 978-0984738212

Author — Only A Guy
Hard Questions About Heaven And Hell
ISBN # 978-0984738243

Author — Only A Guy
Hard Questions about Humanity
ISBN # 978-1939670199

Author — Only A Guy
Hard Questions About Salvation
ISBN # 978-0984738281

Author — Only A Guy
Hope In A Lost And Fallen World
ISBN # 978-0984738250

Author — Only A Guy
Hard Questions About The End Times
ISBN # 978-1939670007

Author — Only A Guy
Hard Questions About Angeles And Demons
ISBN # 978-0984738267

NOW AVAILABLE
from VIP INK PUBLISHING, L.L.C.

Author—Noces Joseph LaFont, Jr.
Kajun King Trapper Joe's Story
ISBN # 978-1-939670-23-6

Noces Joseph LaFont, Jr. (Trapper Joe) is a veteran when it comes to south Louisiana hunting and fishing. His traditional Cajun roots implanted into him as a child has been show cased on the hit television show Swamp People that airs on the History Channel. Alligator season is the most exciting and most dangerous time of the year for alligator hunters in Louisiana. When Trapper Joe is not hunting alligators, he is hunting for other game within the Cajun lifestyle such as: fish, crawfish, shrimp, crabs,raccoons, turtles, deer, hog, rabbit, dove and so forth. His autobiography details his life from growing up in south Louisiana to helping Swamp People become the #1 rated reality show on the History channel with a premiere viewing of 3.1 million. It is filled with amazing hunting and fishing stories as well as his Cajun recipes. This book is a real must have for any true fan of the Cajun lifestyle.

NOW AVAILABLE
from VIP INK PUBLISHING, L.L.C.

Author—Michael Lewis
Dreams
ISBN # 978-1939670168

Michael Lewis, team ambassador of the New Orleans Saints, is best known as a return specialist. Although Lewis did not play college football, he was signed by the Louisiana Bayou Beast in 1998. Lewis has also played for the New Orleans Thunder, New Jersey Red Dogs, Philadelphia Eagles, New Orleans Saints and San Francisco 49ers. In 2000, Lewis' life would dramatically change as went from a former Budweiser beer truck driver (thus, the nickname "Beer Man") to being signed by the New Orleans Saints practice squad. In 2001, he was sent by the Saints to play for the Rhein Fire of NFL Europe. Later that year, Lewis would begin his career as a New Orleans Saint. In 2002, he would set an NFL record for combined kick-punt return yardage with 2,432 yards total (1,807 kickoff, 625 punt). He is currently the Saints' all-time career leader in punt returns (142) and punt return yardage (1,482). On June 15, 2007, the Saints released him. The local New Orleans newspaper, the Times-Picayune, titled the news, "There's a Tear in My Beer" because he was a local inspiration, who went from beer truck driver to NFL star. Michael Lewis' autobiography covers his life from his humble beginnings to becoming a NFL star. It also covers his faith and determination as well as the struggles he had to face and overcome. His inspiring story will touch the hearts of millions.

NOW AVAILABLE
from VIP INK PUBLISHING, L.L.C.

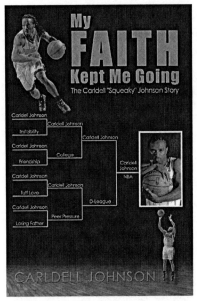

Author—Carldell Johnson
My Faith Kept Me Going
ISBN # 978-1939670113

Johnson's autobiography covers his faith and determination on both on and off the court. It also outlines how he overcame the hardships of living in New Orleans East as a child as well as the horrors he experienced during and after Hurricane Katrina, and his triumph of becoming an NBA player. His inspiring story will touch the hearts of many.

On December 9, 2011 Carldell Johnson signed with the New Orleans Hornets training camp roster, where he became a home town favorite. After he was released from the New Orleans Hornets, Johnson returned to the Austin Toros where they won the NBA Development League Championship. Since turning professional in 2006, he played for three different teams in Mexico and two in Belgium as well as having three different stints with the Austin Toros in the NBA Development League. He also has been a non-roster invitee of the San Antonio Spurs on two occasions. Carldell Johnson also participate with the New York Knicks mini camp in 2012. Later that year he played for the Atlanta Hawks during their 2012 pre-season.

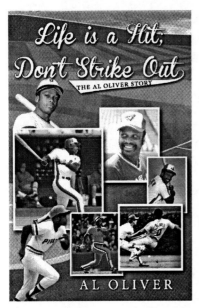

CPSIA information can be obtained
at www.ICGtesting.com
Printed in the USA
FFOW05n2224200916